Sharing Jesus:
He Wanted a Bride

Sharing Jesus:
He Wanted a Bride

By
Amy Zema

For Carol K.

Silver or gold I do not have, but what I do have I give you. Jesus.
(Acts 3:6, NIV)

Table of Contents

Amy Zema

Acknowledgements

Father God for sending Jesus.

Jesus for His obedience.

Holy Spirit for revelation knowledge.

Amy Zema

Introduction

*When Jesus came to the region of Caesarea Philippi, he asked his disciples, "Who do people say that the Son of Man is?" "Well," they replied, "some say John the Baptist, some say Elijah, and others say Jeremiah or one of the other prophets." Then he asked them, "But who do you say I am?" Simon Peter answered, "You are the Messiah, the Son of the living God." Jesus replied, "You are blessed, Simon son of John, because **my Father in heaven has revealed this to you.** You did not learn this from any human being. Now I say to you that you are Peter (which means 'rock'), and upon this rock I will build my church, and all the powers of hell will not conquer it. (Matthew 16:13-18, NLT)*

Jesus asked His disciples, "Who do you say that I am?" Peter answered, "You are the Messiah, the Son of the living God." "Messiah" means the Christ, the one anointed by God the Father to be the Savior of the world.

Jesus told Peter that no man could have revealed to him that Jesus was the Savior of all mankind, but *this* knowledge was revealed to him directly from God the Father. Jesus then declared that He will build His church upon *this* rock. Some religious sects presume that the "rock" was Peter, and hence the first Pope as the head of that church. However, if Jesus would have meant that the church would be built upon Peter, surely He would have stated upon "you" I will build my church, not upon "this." This "rock" Jesus speaks of upon which His church is built is revelation knowledge that comes directly from God the Father.

Imagine building a physical house. The entire structure is supported by a foundation. The first stone set in the foundation is the cornerstone, which determines the position of the entire structure. The "rock" Jesus speaks of, the foundation of His church, is revelation knowledge believers receive from God the Father. Jesus as our Savior is the first truth that God the Father reveals to us, and this truth is the cornerstone of the foundation upon which all knowledge about Jesus and his plan for mankind is built.

In his letter to the Church at Ephesus, Paul explains:

Together, we are his house, built on the foundation of the apostles and the prophets. And the cornerstone is Christ Jesus himself. (Ephesians 2:20, NLT)

In the next chapter, Paul explains that this foundation upon which His church is built is revelation knowledge, revealed to Paul, together with apostles and prophets:

As I briefly wrote earlier, God himself revealed his mysterious plan to me. As you read what I have written, you will understand my insight into this plan regarding Christ. God did not reveal it to previous generations, but now by his Spirit he has revealed it to his holy apostles and prophets. (Ephesians 3:3-5, NLT)

Revelation knowledge about Jesus and His plan for mankind is available to all those who have accepted Jesus as their Lord and Savior. Peter knew that Jesus is the Savior because of revelation knowledge he received directly from God the Father. Peter later stated, *"I now realize how true it is that God does not show favoritism...."* *(Acts 10:34, NLT)*. This revelation knowledge is also available for you.

As you read the Bible, ask the Father to reveal Jesus to you in every book, every chapter, every sentence, and every word. As you read this book, take the time to meditate on the quoted scriptures, and ask Father God to reveal to you personally the truths of His Word.

Amy Zema

Chapter 1
Ask Me

Keep on asking, and you will be given what you ask for. Keep on looking, and you will find. Keep on knocking, and the door will be opened. For everyone who asks, receives. Everyone who seeks, finds. And the door is opened to everyone who knocks. (Matthew 7:7-8, NLT)

The world is full of lost people who have faced lifetimes of disappointments, leaving them with a painful knowledge of a void within, and an instinctive knowing that something is missing from their lives. This "instinctive knowing" comes directly from God:

For the truth about God is known to them instinctively. God has put this knowledge in their hearts. From the time the world was created, people have seen the earth and sky and all that God made. They can clearly see his invisible qualities— his eternal power and divine nature. (Romans 1:19-20, NLT)

Those of us who love Jesus know that He is what is missing from their lives, and He is the only way to fill that void that burns within. We may tell others about Jesus, but may be unable to answer questions they have, or share Him in a life-transforming way. The ultimate questions burning in their souls might be: What is the purpose of life? Why was man created? Why did Jesus have to die? Knowing the answers to these questions enables a Christian to present Jesus to others in a simple yet effective way that would show that He is what is missing in their lives, and only He can fill that void within.

Over the years, I have learned many formulas to follow, many program steps to take, and many methods of praying, but I still could not share Jesus with others in an effective and life transforming way. I realized that these programs, steps, and methods caused me to take my eyes off the simplicity of Jesus. I threw away all the devices I had learned, and instead embraced the same determination as Paul:

> *For I am determined not to know any thing among you except Jesus Christ, and Him crucified. (1Corinthians 2:2, NKJV)*

Numbers 23:19 tell us that, *"God is not a man that he should lie."* From this we know that Jesus is a man of His word. Jesus said in Matthew 7:8, *"Everyone who asks, receives...."*

So I asked Him to show me why we were born and why He had to die.
.

He answered, "I wanted a Bride."

Chapter 2
Formed and Fashioned

*And the Lord God formed man of the dust of the
ground, and breathed into his nostrils the breath of
life; and man became a living soul*

....

*And the Lord God said, it is not good that man
should be alone; I will make him an help meet for
him. And out of the ground the Lord God formed
every beast of the field, and every foul of the air....
but for Adam there was not found an help meet for
him.... And the Lord caused a deep sleep to fall
upon Adam, and he slept: and he took one of his
ribs, and closed up the flesh instead thereof;
And the rib, which the Lord God had taken from
man, made he a woman, and brought her unto the
man. And Adam said, This is now bone of my bones
and flesh of my flesh: she shall be called Woman,
because she was taken out of Man. Therefore shall
a man leave his father and his mother, and shall
cleave unto his wife: and they shall become one
flesh (Genesis 2:7, 18-24, KJV)*

The first love story is recorded in the second chapter of
Genesis. God gave Adam the woman named Eve to be his wife,
and the two became one. The Book of Ephesians speaks of this
first union, and reveals that the story of Adam and Eve's marriage
is an illustration of the relationship between Jesus and His church.

*For this cause shall a man leave his father and
mother, and shall be joined unto his wife, and they
two shall be one flesh. This is a great mystery: but I
speak concerning Christ and the church. (Ephesian
5:31-32, KJV)*

3

The Book of Romans further discloses that this picture of Adam in Genesis 2 is an illustration of Jesus: *Now Adam is a symbol, a representation of Christ, who was yet to come (Romans 5:14, NLT).*

Romans and Ephesians sheds a light on the union of Adam with the woman, leading to the following comparison between Adam and Jesus from Genesis 2:

Adam	Jesus
It was not good that man should be alone.	It was not good that Jesus should be alone.
Adam needed a bride.	Jesus wanted a bride.
A created being was not a suitable bride for Adam.	A created being is not a suitable bride for Jesus.
God formed and fashioned Eve *from* Adam as his counterpart and equal; she was not created from the ground.	Jesus needs a bride to be formed and fashioned *from* Him, not created by Him, to become His counterpart and equal.

The Book of Colossians reveals Jesus as the creator of the universe:

> *For by him were all things created, that are in heaven, and that are in earth, visible and invisible, whether they be thrones, or dominions, or principalities, or powers: all things were created by him, and for him.(Colossians 1:16, NLT)*

Jesus created man. Isaiah makes it abundantly clear that a creation can never be equal to its creator:

> *How foolish can you be? He is the Potter, and he is certainly greater than you, the clay! Should the created thing say of the one who made it, "He didn't make me"? Does a jar ever say, "The potter who made me is stupid"? (Isaiah 29:16, NLT)*

Just as Adam needed a counterpart, an equal as his bride, so Jesus wants a counterpart, an equal for His bride. Man, a created being, has never been suitable as a bride for Jesus, the creator. **Jesus' bride must be formed and fashioned *from* Him, not created by Him.**

How did Jesus form and fashion His bride?

God came to earth as a created man: *He took the humble position of a slave and was born as a human being. (Philippians 2:7, NLT).* But when Jesus was resurrected from the dead, a miraculous change took place. Jesus was born again as a brand new being with a glorified body. He was no longer a created man, but *the image of the invisible God...the firstborn from the dead (Colossians 1:15,18 KJF).* If Jesus is the "first", then there is a second, third, fourth, etc. We are those people.

When we choose Jesus, He gives us His Holy Spirit to live in us. *Don't you realize that your body is the temple of the Holy Spirit, who lives in you and was given to you by God? (1 Corinthians 6:19, NLT).* Our inner man, our spirit, is born again, and we are then fashioned *from* Jesus. However, we remain as Jesus did during His earthly ministry, part God because of the indwelling of the Holy Spirit, and part created man because of our physical bodies. At the second coming of Jesus when He returns to the earth for His bride, we will receive glorified bodies, the same as Jesus the firstborn received when He was resurrected from the dead. **We will no longer be *created* beings, but brand new beings formed and fashioned *from* Jesus Himself, His counterpart, His equal, His Bride.**

> *Behold, I shew you a mystery; we shall not all sleep, but we shall all be changed, in a moment, in the twinkling of an eye, at the last trump: for the trumpet shall sound, and the dead shall be raised*

incorruptible, and we shall be changed. (1 Corinthians 15:51-52, KJV)

He wanted a Bride.

Chapter 3
The Bible: His Story, Our History

Every book of the Bible, from Genesis to Revelation, reveals Jesus. It is His story, our history, written by the apostles and prophets, inspired by the Holy Spirit.

Jesus told the Jews that the Bible is His story:

You search the Scriptures, for in them you think you have eternal life; and these are they which testify of Me. (John 5:39, NKJV)

Jesus revealed His story to the men on the road to Emmaus:

And beginning at Moses and all the prophets He expounded to them in all the Scriptures the things concerning Himself. (Luke 24:27, NKJV)

Jesus caused the Apostles to understand His story:

Then he (Jesus) said, "When I was with you before I told you that everything written about me by Moses and the prophets and the Psalms must come true." Then he opened their minds to understand these many Scriptures. (Luke 24:44-45, NLT)

Phillip testified to his brother Nathaniel:

We have found Him of whom Moses in the law, and also the prophets wrote-- Jesus of Nazareth, the son of Joseph. (John 1:45, NKJV)

It is believed that the original text of the Bible was written in Hebrew. The dispersion of the Jews from their homeland over the centuries caused them to eventually forget the language of their ancestors, and Greek became their dominant language. During the third century the Jews undertook the translation of the Hebrew

Scriptures into Greek, known as the *Septuagint*. Given the Jews strong heritage and belief in the Covenants between God and their forefathers, the books of the Bible were divided into two distinct units known as the "Old Covenant" and the "New Covenant."

During the fourth century the Christian faith dominated the Roman Empire, and Pope Damasus commissioned a leading biblical scholar named Jerome to translate the Bible into Latin. The Latin *Vulgate,* as it became known, divided the books of the Bible into the "Old Testament" being the time before the birth of Jesus, and the "New Testament" being the time after Jesus was born. Throughout the ensuing centuries there were many more translations of the Bible, resulting in Bible scholars debating over the Biblical use of the word "testament" as opposed to the word "covenant." The contemporary versions of the Bible use these words interchangeably, but they are not exactly the same.

A "covenant" is an agreement between two living parties which provides that if specific conditions are met, certain promises will be fulfilled. Who did God covenant with in the "Old Testament?" On the other hand, a "testament" is a written document providing for the disposition of a person's property after death to an heir. Who is the person writing their last will and testament in the "New Testament?" Both translations of the Bible overlap, and both covenant and testament are fulfilled in the Bible. The Bible is the history of mankind, our history, recording both a covenant and a testament. The two divisions of the Bible can be more accurately thought of as the Old Covenant with Mankind seen through Moses and the Prophets, and the New Covenant and Last Will and Testament of Jesus Christ.

The "Old Testament" is the covenant between God and Man, seen through the patriarchs, including Noah, Abraham,

Moses and David. However, none of these men, nor any man on earth, was able to fulfill the conditions of the covenant between God and Man. And then came Jesus.

Jesus is the only man that was able to satisfy the conditions of the covenant between God and Man:

> *Don't misunderstand why I have come. I did not come to abolish the Law of Moses or the writings of the prophets. No, I came to fulfill them. (Matthew 5:17, NLT)*

Jesus' obedience caused Him to satisfy the terms and conditions of the covenant between God and Man. He therefore became the only beneficiary of all the covenant promises found in the "Old Testament."

Jesus now offers us these promises in a new covenant:

> *He took the cup of wine after supper, saying, "This cup is the new covenant between God and his people--an agreement confirmed with my blood...."* *(1 Corinthians 11:25, NLT)*

And our only condition is that we believe in Jesus:

> *For God loved the world so much that he gave his one and only Son, so that everyone who believes in him will not perish but have eternal life. (John 3:16, NLT)*

The men and women who satisfy the only condition of the New Covenant by simply believing in Jesus are now named in His Book of Life as the beneficiaries of Jesus' Last Will and Testament:

> *All who are victorious will be clothed in white. I will never erase their names from the Book of Life, but I will announce before my Father and his angels that they are mine. (Revelation 3:5, NLT)*

Those "clothed in white" who are the heirs of Jesus' Last Will and Testament, are revealed to be His Bride:

> *For the time has come for the wedding feast of the Lamb, and his bride has prepared herself. She has been given the finest of pure white linen to wear. (Revelation 19:7-8, NLT)*

And the New Covenant Last Will and Testament of Jesus Christ appoints all the promises found in the "Old Testament" as an unconditional free gift, an unconditional New Covenant, to those that believe in Him, His Bride: *And I appoint unto you a kingdom as My Father has appointed unto me. (Luke 22:29, King James).*

Come with me now as God reveals to us more about His Bride. *Come with me! I will show you the bride, the wife of the Lamb.* (Revelation 21:9, NLT)

Chapter 4
The Last Chapter

For the time is coming when everything that is covered will be revealed, and all that is secret will be made known to all. (Matthew 10:26, NLT)

A plot can be defined as a secret plan to accomplish a purpose. In the literary sense, the plot of a novel is a sequence of events that revolve around the efforts of the main character to solve a problem and attain a goal. In the last chapter of a novel, all secrets are revealed, and the goal is accomplished.

Jesus' literary masterpiece known as *The Bible* opens with the conflict of God's separation from His fallen man, recorded in the Book of Genesis, and ends with the reuniting of man and God, revealing mankind's destiny as the Bride of Christ, chronicled in the last chapter of the Bible, the Book of Revelation.

Jesus' story begins with the creation of man in the Garden of Eden:

In the beginning, God created the heaven and the earth.... So God created man in his own image, in the image of God He created him; male and female He created them. (Genesis 1:1, 27 NKJV)

The story of God goes on to tell us of the fall of the man Adam, who was created in God's own image, and the near destruction of the earth by a flood where only one man named Noah and his family were saved. The story continues with Abraham, a man whom God called His friend, and the deliverance of this man's family from the cruel bonds of slavery. Next is the story of Kings and priests ruling, guiding and directing man, and the Prophets foretelling of the coming Messiah, the deliverer, the Savior of man. God goes on to tell of the arrival of Jesus, the Messiah, here on the corrupted, dying earth where He once walked long ago with man in the cool of the day, only to be betrayed and put to death by the man He created in His image and likeness, the man that was unequaled in His glorious creation, the man He called "very good." And finally, God's story climaxes telling of Jesus' resurrection from the dead into everlasting life.

And so is the story, the history of God, and as with any good story or book, all is revealed in the last chapter. Therein lies the reason man was created, the very purpose of man's life. The entire Bible, the entire history of God, comes to its culmination, its glorious crescendo, in the Book of the Revelation of Jesus Christ:

> *For the marriage of the lamb is come, and His wife*
> *has made herself ready. (Revelation 19:7, NKJV)*

The desire of Jesus' heart is to have a wife.

The Bible resounds with the wedding theme, from the Garden of Eden in Genesis to the City of God in Revelation.

In Genesis, one man became two people, who in turn became one flesh:

> *Therefore shall a man leave his father and his mother, and*
> *be joined to his wife, and they shall be one flesh. (Genesis*
> *2:24, NKJV)*

Paul revealed to the Ephesians that this great mystery is all about Jesus and His church:

> *This is a great mystery, but I speak concerning*
> *Christ and the church. (Ephesians 5:32, NKJV)*

He told the Corinthians that he espoused them to Jesus and wanted them pure for the wedding:

I am jealous for you with the jealousy of God himself. For I promised you as a pure bride to one husband, Christ. (2 Corinthians 11:2, NLT)

John casts away any doubt when he witnesses the thundering voices in Heaven crying that the wedding of the Lamb has come and His Bride has made herself ready:

For the time has come for the wedding feast of the Lamb, and his bride has prepared herself. She has been given the finest of pure white linen to wear. (Revelation 19:7-8, NLT)

His Story, from the creation of mankind in the image of God through the marriage supper of the Lamb, is all about the Bridegroom uniting with His Bride.

And as the bridegroom rejoices over the bride, so shall your God rejoice over you. (Isaiah 62:5, NKJV)

He wanted a Bride.

Chapter 5
The Betrothal

I will betroth you to me forever; I will betroth you in righteousness and justice, in love and compassion. (Hosea 2:19, NIV)

The term "betrothal" in Jewish law is more than just a promise of a man and woman to marry. Once a man and a woman are betrothed, the union is definite and binding upon both parties, who were considered as man and wife in all legal and religious aspects, with the actual exception of cohabitating with one another.

The ancient Jewish marriage customs are magnificently correlated in the Bible leading to the wedding supper of the Lamb, foreshadowing what is and what is to come.

In ancient Israel, a bride was chosen by the father of the bridegroom. Likewise, we were chosen by Father God:

Even before he made the world, God loved us and chose us in Christ to be holy and without fault in his eyes. (Ephesians 1:4, NLT).

You didn't choose me. I chose you. (John 15:16, NLT)

Once the bride was chosen, the father of the bride would be presented with three things: the bridegroom's best financial offer, a marriage contract, and a skin of wine. These three distinct parts of the Jewish marriage customs are clearly depicted in the Bible revealing Jesus' betrothal to His bride.

THE BRIDEGROOM'S BEST FINANCIAL OFFER

The Jewish custom was to purchase the bride with the best financial offering the bridegroom could afford.

When Abraham sought a wife for his son Isaac, he instructed his servant to present his best financial offer as the price for the bride: *He loaded ten of Abrahams' camels with gifts and set out, taking with him the best of everything his master owned. (Genesis 24:10, NLT).* Rebekah was betrothed to Isaac, and the bride price was paid: *Then the servant brought out gold silver jewelry and articles of clothing and gave them to Rebekah; he also gave costly gifts to her brother and mother. (Genesis 24:53, NLT).*

Isaac's son Jacob chose Rachel as his wife, but first spent seven years working for her father to pay the requisite bride price: *Since Jacob was in love with Rachel, he told her father, "I'll work for you for seven years if you'll give me Rachel, your younger daughter, as my wife." "Agreed," Laban replied. "I'd rather give her to you then to someone outside of the family." So Jacob spent the next seven years to pay for Rachel. (Genesis 29:18-20, NLT).*

The price paid for the Bride of Christ was not corruptible things like the gold and silver that was paid by the biblical patriarchs. Instead, Father God gave the blood of His precious Son, the Bridegroom, as the purchased price for Jesus' Bride, for you.

> *You were not redeemed with corruptible things like silver or gold.... He paid for you with the precious lifeblood of Christ, the sinless, spotless Lamb of God. God chose him for this purpose long before the world began, but now in these final days, he was sent to the earth for all to see. And he did this for you. (1 Peter 1:19-20, NLT)*

THE MARRIAGE CONTRACT

The father of the bridegroom would also bring a *Ketubah*, a written contract which contains the marriage promises outlining the groom's obligation to the bride. *Ketubah* means *it is written*, and can be likened to a prenuptial agreement. The traditional text of the *Ketubah* provides: "I will work for thee, honor, provide for, and support thee, in accordance with the practice of Jewish husbands, who work for their wives, honor, provide for and support them in truth." The bridegroom is obligated to feed his bride, clothe her, provide her conjugal needs, pay her medical bills, ransom her if she is taken hostage, and pay her burial expense. The promises of *our Ketubah* as the Bride of Christ are found in the written Word of God.

The Old Testament prophet Isaiah identifies the Bridegroom, our husband, the one who paid the bride price:

> *For your Maker is your husband, the Lord of hosts is His name; and your Redeemer is the Holy One of Israel; He is called the God of the whole earth. (Isaiah 54:5, NKJV).*

The prophet Hosea looks to a time in his future and reveals the Bridegroom's intention toward His chosen bride:

> *I will make you my wife forever, showing you righteousness and justice, unfailing love and compassion. I will be faithful to you and make you mine, and you will finally know me as Lord. (Hosea 2:15, 20 NLT)*

One of His greatest *Ketubah* promises to His Bride is the promise of peace:

> *For the mountains shall depart and the hills be removed, but my kindness shall not depart from you, nor shall the covenant of my peace be removed.... (Isaiah 54:10, NKVJ)*

Peace is not merely a feeling of contentment, but a complete and full provision. The Hebrew word for peace is *shalom*, which includes safety, provision, health and prosperity. These are the very promises to the bride found in the ancient *Ketubah*. The promise of peace establishes the bride in righteousness, free from oppression, fear and terror. No weapon shall ever come against the bride, not even a word spoken against her.

> *In righteousness you shall be established; you shall be far from oppression; for you shall not fear; and from terror, for it shall not come near you.*
>
> . . .
>
> *No weapon formed against you shall prosper; and every tongue that rises against you in judgment you shall condemn. This is the heritage of the servants of the Lord, and their righteousness is from Me, says the Lord. (Isaiah 54:14, 17 NKJV)*

The financial offering and the marriage contract were presented to the bride's father for his approval. Peter makes it clear that God is the Father of the Bridegroom: *All praise to God, the Father of our Lord Jesus Christ (1 Peter 1:3, NLT);* and that we too become His children because of our faith in Jesus: *For you are children of God through faith in Christ Jesus (Galatians 3:26).* However, the question arises in the context of the *Ketubah*, if God is the Father of Jesus the Bridegroom, and we are the Bride of Christ, who is the father of the Bride? The apostle Paul answers that if we have the same kind of faith that the Old Testament patriarch Abraham had, then he is the father of us all:

> *Therefore, the promise is based on faith so that it can be a gift. Consequently, the promise is guaranteed for every descendant, not only for those who are descendants by obeying Moses' Teachings*

*but also for those who are descendants **by believing**
as Abraham did. **He is the father of all of us.**
(Romans 4:16, GWT).*

It is not what Abraham did or even his obedience to God
that made him righteous in God's eyes. But it was simply that he
believed God.

*And so it happened just as the Scriptures say:
"Abraham believed God, and God counted him as
righteous **because of his faith**." He was even called
the friend of God. (James 2:23, NLT)*

Abraham is the father of the bride, the one to whom was
presented the bride price and marriage contract. Abraham
accepted the *Ketubah* promise of marriage, and Jesus himself tells
us that Abraham looked forward to the day that the Bridegroom
would come:

*Your father Abraham rejoiced to see my day: and
he saw it, and was glad. (John 8:56, KJV)*

If you have the same faith as Abraham, if you simply
believe, then Abraham is indeed your "father," and you are the
Bride betrothed to God's Son, the Bridegroom.

*Understand, then, that those who have faith are
children of Abraham. Scripture foresaw that God
would justify the Gentiles by faith, and announced
the gospel in advance to Abraham: "All nations will
be blessed through you." So those who rely on faith
are blessed along with Abraham, the man of faith.
(Galatians 3:7-9, NIV)*

THE SKIN OF WINE

The betrothal is completed with the offering of a cup of
wine to the chosen bride. The father of the bridegroom chose the

bride, and brought the financial offering and the *Ketubah* to the bride's father. They discussed the details of where they would live, how the son would provide for the daughter, and the price the son's father would pay. But only the bride herself could pick up the cup of wine and drink it. Only she could agree to become his wife. Jesus set that cup before His disciples the night He was betrayed and offered it to them to drink. Jesus offered the same cup to you when you accepted Him as your Lord and Savior.

Just as a bride is given the choice to accept the proposal, so are we given that choice. John tells us that God is love, and his love is manifested towards us through Jesus:

> *He who does not love does not know God, or God is love. In this the love of God was manifested toward us, that God has sent His only begotten Son into the world, that we might live through Him. (I John 4:8-9, NKJV)*

What you must understand, however, is that although God loves us unconditionally, no matter what, love is not complete until it is returned. God does not force us to love Him in return. It is a choice, just as the Jewish bride made the choice by drinking from the cup offered to her. All throughout His story, He has given man a choice. He set the tree of knowledge before Adam, and man was given a choice. God set the choice between life and death before the Israelites, and implored them to choose life:

> *I have set before you life and death, blessing and cursing: therefore choose life, that both you and your descendants may live. (Deuteronomy 30:19, KJV)*

Joshua declared to those in the wilderness that he and his family chose to serve the Lord:

And if it seem evil to you to serve the Lord, choose for yourselves this day whom you will serve, whether the gods which your fathers served that were on the other side of the River, or the gods of the Amorites, in whose land you dwell. Bu as for me and my house, we will serve the Lord. (Joshua 24:15, NKJV)

Even Mary the sister of Martha had a choice, and Jesus said she chose the "good part":

Now it happened as they went that he entered into a certain village; and a certain woman named Martha welcomed him into her house. And she had a sister called Mary, who also sat at Jesus' feet, and heard his word. But Martha was distracted with much serving, and she approached him and said, Lord, do you not care that my sister has left me to serve alone? Therefore tell her to help me. And Jesus answered and said to her, Martha, Martha, you are worried and troubled about many things: But one thing is needed, and Mary has chosen that good part, which will not be taken away from her. (Luke 10:380-42, NKJV)

God's love is shown to us through Jesus:

In this the love of God was manifested toward us, that God has sent his only begotten Son into the world, that we might live through him. (I John 4:9, NKJV) ·

But God has given us the choice to love Him in return. The marriage covenant, the *Ketubah*, contains all the great and precious promises of the bridegroom to the bride. However, these promises are for the bride that loves Him in return. *"No eye has seen, no ear has heard, and no mind has imagined what God has prepared for those who love Him" (1 Corinthians 2:9, NLT).* But read on!

21

If you love Him in return, God will reveal these promises to you, His bride: *But it was to us that God revealed these things by His Spirit... (1 Corinthians 2:10, NLT).*

A PLACE FOR THE BRIDE

Once the marriage covenant was sealed, the Jewish bridegroom left the bride to go to his father's house to prepare a room where they could go. Our Bridegroom has gone to prepare a wedding chamber for His Bride:

> Jesus said, *"In my Father's house are many mansions: If it were not so, I would have told you. I go to prepare a place for you. And if I go and prepare a place for you, I will come again and receive you to myself, that where I am, there you may be also." (John 14:2-3, NKJV)*

However, it was the bridegroom's father who decided when it was time to go for the bride. And only Father God knows the time when Jesus will return for His Bride:

> *But of that day and hour no one knows, not even the angels in heaven, nor the Son, but only the Father. (Mark 13:32, NKJV)*

When the groom's father decided everything was in place and released his son to bring his bride, a shofar was blown to announce his coming:

> *It will happen in a moment, in the blink of an eye, when the last trumpet is blown. For when the trumpet sounds, those who have died will be raised to live forever. And we who are living will also be transformed. (1 Corinthians 15:52, NLT)*
> *For the Lord himself shall descend from heaven with a shout, with the voice of the archangel, and with the trump of God: and the dead in Christ shall*

rise first: Then we which are alive and *remain shall be caught up together with them in the clouds, to meet the Lord in the air: and so shall we ever be with the Lord. (1 Thessalonians 4:16-17, KJV)*

Chapter 6
The Bride

Come with me! I will show you the bride, the wife of the Lamb. (Revelation 21:9, NLT)

The Jewish father chose the woman who would be the bride to his son. He made the proposal of marriage to the father of the chosen one, presenting him with his best offering and the *Ketubah*. Once the proposal was accepted, only the woman herself could agree to become the son's wife. The cup of wine was placed before her, she would take the cup and drink, sealing the marriage covenant. The father and son would return home to prepare a place where the bride and groom would enjoy the fruits of their marriage. It was the father's decision when the marriage ceremony would take place. Only the father knew of the time.

In the meantime, the bride would make herself ready, spending her days beautifying her appearance and purifying her heart. She would keep a lamp by her bed in case her groom returned for her in the night. Suddenly one day, she would hear the sound of the shofar, the blowing of the horn, to announce that the bridegroom has come for her, to announce that *the marriage of the lamb is come, and his wife has made herself ready. (Revelation 19:7, KJV).*

The Bible is the story of God, His love story with us. He reveals Himself to us through the people, events, poetry, words and imagery of the Bible. In his letter to the Ephesians, Paul quotes Genesis 2:24 concerning the union of Adam and Eve:

For this reason a man shall leave his father and mother and be joined to his wife, and the two shall become one flesh. (Ephesians 5:31, NKJV)

25

He then reveals to us that this great mystery is about Jesus Christ and His Church, His Bride:

> *This is a great mystery, but I speak concerning Christ and the church. (Ephesians 5:32, NKJV)*

Paul speaks to the Corinthians and compares the church to a wife, to Eve:

> *For I am jealous for you with godly jealousy. For I have betrothed you to one husband, that I may present you as a chaste virgin to Christ. But I fear, lest somehow, as the serpent deceived Eve by his craftiness, so your minds may be corrupted from the simplicity that is in Christ. (2 Corinthians 11: 2-3, NJK)*

The history of the creation of the man Adam and his union with the woman Eve, is a picture of the Church and our union with Jesus.

First, there was the creation of man. God created man in His own image, after His own likeness: *And God said, Let us make man in our image, after our likeness... (Genesis 1:26, KJV).*

The Hebrew word for "image" is *tsehlem,* which is a masculine noun. The Hebrew word for "likeness is *demuth,* which is a feminine noun. God fashioned and formed the physical shape and appearance of the first created man Adam as a shadow of Himself, having both the masculine and feminine attributes of God.

Next, was the union of man and woman. God then looked upon Adam and said it was not good for him to be alone, and He would make Adam a "help meet," a companion, a bride. He brought before him all the living things He had created, but among them was not found a suitable wife for him.

And the LORD God said, It is not good that the man should be alone; I will make him an help meet for him. And out of the ground the LORD God formed every beast of the field, and every fowl of the air... but for Adam there was not found an help meet for him. (Genesis 2:18-20, KJV)

Surely God knew that no animal was a suitable help meet. No *created* being was suitable to be Adam's wife. Perhaps He wanted Adam to realize this too, and to place in Adam's heart the desire for a counterpart, one exactly like him, his help meet, his equal, his bride.

Eve, the bride, was not formed from the dust of the ground. She was not a created being. God fashioned and formed the bride from Adam, bone of his bones and flesh of his flesh:

And Adam said, This is now bone of my bones, and flesh of my flesh: she shall be called Woman, because she was taken out of Man. (Genesis 2:23, KJV)

As Eve was *formed* to be Adam's *help meet*, so every believer that makes up the church is *formed* to become Jesus' *help meet*. The word *help meet* is a translation from the Hebrew word *ezer kenegdo*. The translation *help meet* does not adequately describe the richness, beauty, and promises of the original Hebrew word.

The word *helper* used in the English Bible conveys the image of someone subservient who is there to merely offer assistance if needed. The Hebrew word *ezer* has a far different connotation than one who merely aids. It is often used in the Bible describing God as Israel's helper. *Ezer* is a military word, describing a desperately needed ally. God used the word to describe Eve. However, He modified it with the word *kenegdo*, a

27

word used only in Genesis to describe Adam's bride. The word *kenegdo* means counterpart, one who necessarily completes the other. Adam was created in the image and likeness of God. His appearance was the same, his natural body was a reflection of God's, but the woman was formed as the man's counterpart. The woman was taken out of the man; the woman existed as a part of man; the woman was a part of man necessary to make him complete. The only suitable *help meet* for Adam was one that was part of him, one that together with him made him complete. Eve was Adam's *ezer kenegdo*, his magnificent and powerful counterpart.

Eve was not a created being, but she existed as part of Adam, she was then taken out of him, and was formed by God to be Adam's bride. Paul reveals to the Ephesians that this picture of the husband and wife is simply a representation of Jesus and His church:

> *For this cause shall a man leave his father and mother, and shall be joined unto his wife, and they two shall be one flesh. This is a great mystery: but I speak concerning Christ and the church. (Ephesians 5:31-32, KJV)*

Like Adam, Jesus desires an *ezer kenegdo*, a counterpart, an equal, upon whom He can lavish His love. Our destiny is to no longer be a created being. Our destiny is to become a new being, taken out of Jesus, and fashioned from the Son, by the Holy Spirit, to be Jesus' Bride.

Chapter 7
Fashioned From the Son

The LORD God fashioned into a woman the rib which He had taken from the man, and brought her to the man. (Genesis 2:22, NASB)

What would it be like if Adam never sinned? Would we still be living in the Garden of Eden? At the end of the ages will life be restored to what it was for Adam in the paradise of God?

As wonderfully glorious as the earth must have been when Adam walked in the cool of the day with the Lord, returning to the Garden is not the destiny of the Church. Our *Ketubah* promises us infinitely so much more.

God created Adam in His own image and likeness, but the created man was not, nor ever could have been, God's *ezer kenegdo*, His counterpart, His equal, His Bride. Likewise, God said it was not good for man to be alone, but no *created* being was suitable to be his equal:

> *And Adam gave names to all cattle, and to the fowl of the air, and to every beast of the field; but for Adam there was not found an help meet for him."*
> *Genesis 2:20 (KJV)*

Simply, a creation is subservient to its creator. A creation has never been the counterpart of or equal to its creator. Israel exhorts woe to the creation that makes an attempt at equality by questioning the creator:

> *What sorrow awaits those who argue with their Creator. Does a clay pot argue with its maker? Does the clay dispute with the one who shapes it,*

saying, 'Stop, you're doing it wrong!' Does the pot exclaim, 'How clumsy can you be?' Isaiah 45:9.

Paul affirmed this through the same imagery when asking:

Who are you, a mere human being, to argue with God? Should the thing that was created say to the one who created it, 'Why have you made me like this?' (Romans 9:20, NLT).

Adam was created from the dust of the ground, a flesh and blood being. Paul makes it certain that a created man could never have been Jesus' *ezer kenegdo*, inheriting the *Ketubah* promises:

What I am saying, dear brothers and sisters, is that our physical bodies cannot inherit the Kingdom of God. These dying bodies cannot inherit what will last forever. (1 Corinthians 15:50, NLT)

There is no reading between the lines or different meaning that can be made from such a simple statement. A flesh and blood man, a created being, could never have been God's *ezer kenegdo*, inheriting the Kingdom of God, the *Ketubah* promises.

The Bible reveals Adam as a pattern or picture foreshadowing Jesus Christ who would be coming in the future:

Now Adam is a symbol, a representation of Christ, who was yet to come. (Romans 5:14, NLT)

The Adam we meet in Genesis 2 is a foreshadowing of Jesus, but he was a created being. The resurrected Jesus, the "last Adam" is not a created being, but a spirit that gives us life:

The first man, Adam, became a living person." But the last Adam--that is, Christ--is a life-giving Spirit. (1 Corinthians 15:45, NLT)

The life that He gives is a new life, fashioning us as a new being.

Just as we are now like Adam, the man of the earth, so we will someday be like Christ, the man from heaven. (1 Corinthians 15:49, NLT)

Just like Adam is a picture or pattern of Jesus, Eve is a pattern or shadow of that new life, the Church, the Bride of Christ.

Adam is a pattern of Christ	Eve is a pattern of the Church, the Bride of Christ
Adam was put to sleep so that Eve could be taken out of his side.	Jesus was "put to sleep" when he died and was buried, so that the Church would be born on Pentecost
Eve was taken out of Adam's side.	At Jesus death, blood and water flowed from his side.
Eve was bone of Adam's bone and flesh of his flesh.	*For we are members of his body, of his flesh, and of his bones. Ephesians 5:30*
Eve was presented by the Father to Adam as his bride, pure and without sin.	We will be presented to Jesus as His Bride, *without spot or wrinkle...holy and without fault. Ephesians 5:27*
Adam and Eve became one flesh. (Genesis 2:24)	Paul refers to Genesis 2:24 and states: *I speak concerning Christ and the Church. Ephesians 5:32*

Genesis 2 uses two different Hebrew words to describe when God created Adam and when He fashioned Eve. Adam was created from the dust of the ground:

And the LORD God formed man of the dust of the ground, and breathed into his nostrils the breath of life; and man became a living soul. (Genesis 2:7, KJV)

The Hebrew word for "formed" used in this passage is *yatsar,* which means to form as a potter forms his clay. Eve, however, was not created from the dust of the ground, but she was fashioned from the rib which God had taken from the man.

> *And the rib, which the LORD God had taken from man, made he a woman, and brought her unto the man. (Genesis 2:22, KJV)*

The Hebrew word for "made" used in this passage is *banah* used for building temples, palaces, cities and altars. The same word is also used to describe how a child is fashioned in a mother's womb.

God did not create Eve from the dust of the ground, but fashioned her from Adam, bone of his bones and flesh of his flesh. Adam's *ezer kenegdo* was not a created being. She was fashioned from him. Likewise, the Son of God's *ezer kenegdo* could not be a created being. She would have to be one formed, fashioned from the Son himself.

There is only one way that man can become the Bride of the Son of God, His *ezer kenegdo*, His counterpart, His equal, receiving all the promises of the *Ketubah*, inheriting the Son's very Kingdom. Jesus revealed the way to Nicodemus: *Except a man be born again, he cannot inherit the kingdom of God. (John 3:3, KJV)*. Flesh and blood, the created being, cannot inherit the Kingdom of God. Adam could not have inherited the Kingdom of God. Adam needed Jesus as much as we do. He was created, *yatsar*. A created being could never be equal with the creator. Man needed to be fashioned, formed, *banah,* from the Creator Himself to be His counterpart, His Bride.

To believe that if Adam had never sinned we would still be in the Garden of Eden, or to believe that we will someday be restored to the life Adam lived in the Garden, is an insult to God and His Son. Adam needed Jesus as much as we do today. Although he walked and talked with Him in the cool of the day,

Adam, a created being, could not have inherited Jesus' Kingdom because he was a flesh and blood man.

God's plan for redemption through the death of Jesus on the cross was not an afterthought regarding Adam's sin. Jesus was not God's "Plan B."

He wanted a Bride.

Chapter 8
Jesus Was Not "Plan B"

In hope of eternal life, which God, that cannot lie, promised before the world began. (Titus 1:2, KVJ)

Jesus' purpose in coming to the earth as a man was not to restore sinful man to the position Adam had in the Garden of Eden. It is unimaginable to think that if Adam would not have sinned, we would not need Jesus. Jesus was not God's Plan B. Scripture reveals that Jesus was *the lamb slain before the foundation of the world (Revelation 13:8, KVJ)*. Paul tells us in Acts that *known unto God are all His works form the beginning of the world (Acts 15:8, KJV)*. And in *Titus 1:2, before the world began*, God promised eternal life to those who would believe.

The "Plan B" theory has its roots in Genesis 3. After man sinned, God announced to the serpent that beguiled Eve that the seed of the woman would come and bruise his head.

> *And I will put enmity between you and the woman, and between your seed and her Seed; He shall bruise your head, and you shall bruise his heel. (Genesis 3:15, NKJV)*

Many have concluded that this was the first mention of Jesus as God's plan of redemption, as an afterthought following man's sin. However, Jesus coming to the earth as the Christ, the Messiah, the light of mankind, is revealed on the very first day of the creation of the universe:

> *Then God said, 'Let there be light," and there was light....God called the light Day, and the darkness He called Night. So the evening and the morning were the first day. (Genesis 1:3-5, NKJV)*

On the first day, God established light, but this light is not the sun. The sun and the moon were not created until the fourth day:

> *Then God made two great lights; the greater light to rule the day, and the lesser light to rule the night: he made the stars also...So the evening and the morning were the fourth day (Genesis 1:16-19, NKJV)*

So, what "light" did God establish on the first day?

The Apostle John revisits the Book of Genesis, and reveals that Jesus was with God during the creation of the universe, and the light spoken into existence on the first day was the plan of redemption, the bridal plan. Jesus would come to the earth, die, and be the first to be born again; and that through faith in Him, man would no longer be a created being, but would be born again as the counterpart of God, the Bride of Christ. This revelation unfolds in the first chapter of John's gospel:

First, John tells us that Jesus, identified as the Word, was with God from the beginning:

> *In the beginning was the Word, and the Word was with God, and the Word was God....And the Word was made flesh and dwelt among us (John 1:1, 14 NKJV)*

Next, John tells us Jesus' life brought light to mankind:

> *The Word gave life to everything that was created, and His life brought life to everyone. (John 1:1-4, NLT)*

And finally, that light spoken into existence on the first day of creation was the bridal plan-- those who simply believe Jesus are born again, no longer created beings, but are transformed into the counterpart of God, the Bride of Christ:

> *He (John the Baptist) was a witness to the light. The one who is the true light, who gives light to everyone, was going to come into the world... But to all who believed Him and accepted Him, He gave the right to become children of God. They are reborn! This is not a physical birth resulting from human passion or plan—this rebirth comes from God. (John 1:7-13 NLT).*

On the very first day, before the creation of the heavens, God put in place the entire purpose of all that He would create in the next five days. Jesus *was* the very foundation of the world. The light spoken into existence on the first day *was* Jesus as the plan to redeem created mankind, the bridal plan, enabling mankind to become Jesus' Bride at the marriage supper of the Lamb.

> *I am the light of the world. If you follow me, you won't have to walk in darkness, because you will have the light that leads to life. (John 8:12 NKJV)*

Jesus died on the cross and paid the price for the sins of all mankind, giving us the opportunity to be put back into a right relationship with God, and having the ability to walk and talk with Him as Adam did in the Garden of Eden. As wonderful as that is, God planned *even more* for us. If you believe in your heart and confesses with your mouth that Jesus died for your sins, choosing to accept Jesus as your Lord and Savior, you are thereby accepting the *Ketubah* marriage cup offered to the Bride:

> *That if you confess with your mouth the Lord Jesus and believe in your heart that God has raised him from the dead, you will be saved. (Romans 10:9, NKJV)*

At the point of acceptance, the *created* man and his nature to sin die, and he or she becomes born again by the same Spirit which raised Jesus from the dead. Jesus' very Spirit now dwells in the born again man or woman who is no longer a *created* being, but formed and fashioned from Jesus Himself, His *ezer kenegdo*, His equal, His counterpart, His bride.

Jesus explained to Nicodemus the necessity of being born again:

> *Jesus replied, 'I assure you, unless you are born again you can never see the Kingdom of God.' 'What do you mean?' exclaimed Nicodemus. 'How can an old man go back into his mother's womb and be born again?' Jesus relied, 'The truth is, no one can enter the Kingdom of God without being born of water and the Spirit. Humans can reproduce only human life, but the Holy Spirit gives new life from heaven. So don't be surprised at my statement that you must be born again. (John 3:3-6, NLT)*

Jesus was not God's plan B. God promised Jesus to us even before the world began. Paul shared this truth with Titus:

> *In hope of eternal life, which God, that cannot lie, promised before the world began (Titus 1:2)*

And John explains that eternal life *is* Jesus:

> *For you granted him authority over all people that he might give eternal life to all those you have given him. Now this is eternal life: that they know you, the only true God, and Jesus Christ, whom you have sent. (John 17:2-3, NIV)*

The Hebrew word for "know" used in this passage is *ginosko*, which is also used in the Book of Matthew to describe the intimacy between a husband and wife.

And knew her not till she had brought forth her firstborn son: and he called his name JESUS. (Matthew 1:25, KJV)

Eternal life, promised before the beginning of the world, is having an intimate relationship with Jesus; He as our husband, and we, His church, as His wife.

He wanted a Bride.

Chapter 9
Jesus Is The Beginning

In the beginning God created the heaven and earth.
(Genesis 1:1, NKJV)

God reveals Jesus Christ not only in the prophetic words of Moses and the prophets, but in every book, gospel, chapter, passage, every sentence, and even in the first three words of the Bible: *in the beginning.*

The words "in the beginning" are commonly understood to refer to the beginning of time. The original Hebrew words reveal a much different meaning.

IN THE BEGINNING: JESUS <u>IS</u> THE BEGINNING

The Hebrew word *techillah* is used in the Old Testament to mean the beginning of a period of time, such as the beginning of a growth period (*Amos 7:1*) or the beginning of a barley harvest (*Ruth 1:22*). The word *techillah* is not the Hebrew word used in Genesis when describing the creation of the heavens and the earth.

The Hebrew word used in Genesis 1:1 to describe the creation of the heavens and earth, "in the beginning," is *reshith*. An accurate meaning of this word is found in how it is used in other places in the Old Testament. *Reshith* portrays the beginning of something, such as the beginning of wisdom or knowledge. It is also translated in English as first fruits, as in tithes or offerings. Most notably is the translation of *reshith* as the firstborn son. In Hebrew, the firstborn was the insignia of a man's procreative strength. The word *reshith* was used in describing Jacob's firstborn son:

> *Reuben you are my firstborn, my strength, the very*
> *first son I had.... (Genesis 49:3, GWT)*

And again, in describing the death of the firstborn sons of the Egyptians on the first Passover:

> *He slaughtered every firstborn in Egypt.... (Psalm*
> *78:51, GWT)*

The Hebrew word from which "in the beginning" is translated in Genesis 1:1, *reshith,* portrays something that the English version does not adequately interpret—Jesus, the firstborn Son of God. In the book of Colossians, Paul identifies Jesus as "the beginning:"

> *And he is the head of the body, the church; **he is the***
> ***beginning** and the firstborn from among the dead,*
> *so that in everything he might have the supremacy.*
> *(Colossians 1:18, NIV)*

The heavens and earth were *not* created *in* the beginning of time; the heavens and earth were created *in* Jesus Christ, "*who is the beginning.*"

IN THE BEGINNING: JESUS WAS ONE WITH THE FATHER

These first three words also portray the oneness Jesus has with the Father. In Genesis 1, the Hebrew word *reshit* is preceded by the letter *bet,* which was translated in English as *in the.* The more accurate translation of this Hebrew letter is *oneness.* Jesus Himself explains this *oneness* when He prayed to the Father that we may all be one, as the Father is in Him and He "in the" Father:

> *...that they all may be one, as You, Father, are in*
> *Me, and I in you; that they also may be one in Us.*
> *(John 17:21, NKJV)*

The words "In the beginning God created the heavens and

the earth" found in Genesis 1:1 have a far deeper meaning than what is understood by the English language. The Hebrew words are more adequately understood to mean: *in oneness with God the Father, Jesus, the beginning, created the heaven and earth.* Genesis 1:1 is not speaking of a period of time, but is revealing Jesus Christ to us.

IN THE BEGINNING: GOD KNEW THE END

The revelation further unfolds with the next phrase of the first sentence of the Bible: *God created the heaven and earth.* In the original Hebrew, the letters *Aleph* and *Tav* are positioned before the word "heaven" and before the word "earth." In the Hebrew alphabet, *Aleph* is the first letter, and *Tav* is the last letter. When these letters are combined in this manner, it is not a word, but creates the image of the first, the last, and everything in between. At the instant of creation, God knew and declared the first days of earth, what would happen to it throughout the ages, and what it would become. What it would become is described in the second sentence of the Bible:

> And the earth was without form, and void; and darkness was upon the face of the deep. And the Spirit of God moved upon the face of the waters. (Genesis 1:2, KJV)

The words *without form* do not describe a physical shape of an earth yet to be formed. The Hebrew word used is *tohuw,* meaning chaos, confusion and moral unreality. The same word is used in Isaiah translated as *vanity,* describing a people separated from God and living in sin:

> None calls for justice, nor any pleads for truth: they trust in vanity, and speak lies; they conceive mischief, and bring forth iniquity. (Isaiah 59:4, AKJ).

43

The Hebrew word for *void* is *bohuw*, meaning an empty ruin. Jeremiah uses the phrase *without form and void* to describe an unholy state of the earth and its inhabitants:

> *Destruction upon destruction is cried, for the whole land is plundered. Suddenly my tents are plundered, and my curtains in a moment. How long will I see the standard, and hear the sound of the trumpet? For my people are foolish, they have not known me. They are silly children, and they have no understanding. They are wise to do evil, but to do good they have no knowledge **I beheld the earth, and indeed, it was without form, and void; and the heavens, they had no light.** (Jeremiah 4:20-23 NKJV)*

The words *"tohuw"* and *"bohuw"* are translated in Isaiah as the confusion and emptiness found in the earth:

> *But the pelican and the porcupine shall possess it, also the owl and the raven shall dwell in it. And He shall stretch out over it the line of confusion and the stones of emptiness. (Isaiah 34:11, NKJV).*

The words "without form and void" do not describe the earth at the beginning of creation, but describe what the earth will become without the light of Jesus.

IN THE BEGINNING: GOD PROVIDES A WAY

Another key to understanding Genesis 1:2, and ultimately understanding God's purpose for creating the world and man's eternal destiny, is found in the one small word - "was." The word "was" is an English translation of the Hebrew word *hayah*. The Bible uses this word to indicate a change in status in the past, or a change in status that will take place in the future. Clearly the Lord anticipated the entire history of the earth. He knew that without light, the earth would become void and covered with darkness, and provided from the beginning of creation, a way to save mankind from what Isaiah describes as confusion and emptiness. The "way" to save the earth from this void and darkness is found in the third sentence of the Bible:

> *And God said, 'let there be light,' and there was light. (Genesis 1:3)*

The light spoken of in Genesis 1:3 is Jesus.

> *The Jesus spoke to them saying, '**I am the light of the world**. He who follows me shall not walk in darkness, but have the light of life. (John 8:12, NKJV).*

Genesis 1:3 reveals the plan to redeem man through Jesus Christ, the bridal plan, and that Jesus is the only way to prevent the earth from being void and covered with darkness.

The prophet Isaiah speaks of creation, how God knew what would happen, and how it would be redeemed:

> *Remember the former things of old, for I am God and there is no else, I am God, and there is none like me, declaring the end from the beginning, and from ancient times the things that are not yet done, saying My counsel shall stand, and I will do all my pleasure. (Isaiah 46, 9-10, KJV).*

From the creation of the world, God knew those things that would happen, and declared that His plan and purpose would prevail. God anticipated what would happen to the earth, and the plan to redeem man, the bridal plan, was in place from the beginning of time.

IN THE BEGINNING: GOD CHOSE HIS BRIDE

Paul tells us in Ephesians 1:4 that *before the foundation of the world we were chosen in Him that we should be holy....* It appears the bride is revealed on the first day of creation.

> *And God saw the light that it was good, and God divided the light from the darkness. God called the light Day and the darkness he called Night. (Genesis 1:4-5, KJV)*

This division of light from darkness is not the separation of the daylight hours from the night time hours of a 24 hour day that occurred on the fourth day of creation. So what is the "dividing" that happened on the first day of creation?

The Hebrew word used for "divided" is *badal,* meaning to separate or set apart. The Arabic meaning for the word *badal* is to exchange, signifying something being bought or sold.

Verse 4 describes an exchange that happened, a purchase transaction between a merchant and buyer. Jesus calls us children of the light, whom He purchased with His own blood:

> *While ye have light, believe in the light, that ye may be the children of light. (John 12:36, KJV)*

> *Take heed therefore unto yourselves, and to all the flock, over the which the Holy Ghost hath made you overseers, to feed the church of God, which he hath purchased with his own blood.(Acts 20:28, KJV)*

Peter tells us that Jesus called us out of darkness into the marvelous light, as was described on the first day of creation:

> *But ye are a chosen generation, a royal priesthood, an holy nation, a peculiar people; that ye should shew forth the praises of **him who hath called you out of darkness into his marvelous light....** (1 Peter 2:9, KJV)*

Before the foundation of the world, on the first day of creation, Jesus called for his Bride.

IN THE BEGINNING: THE REIGN OF THE KING

The vision of Jesus and the bridal plan reaches its culmination in the second part of Genesis 1:5: *And the evening and the morning were the first day.* Revelation in verse 5 comes as we look more closely at the original Hebrew text and the picture portrayed by the word "first."

Starting with the evening and passing through to the morning on the first day of creation depicts a passage from the darkness to the light. The Hebrew word translated "first' in Genesis 1:5 describing the first day of creation is mathematically known as a "cardinal number," whereas the Hebrew words "second" through "seventh" describing the subsequent days of creation are known as "ordinal numbers."

These ordinal numbers found when describing days two through seven denote a sequence, enumerating periods of time. However, the cardinal number used to describe the first day of creation denotes magnitude. More specifically, the Hebrew words for "first day" are described using a cardinal number, which is only used in the Bible to denote the reign of a king.

The culmination of God's bridal plan for mankind is revealed on the first day of creation, depicting the reign of Jesus the King, who has passed through the darkness to the glorious light!

IN THE BEGINNING: THE GOSPEL OF JOHN

The apostle John had much to say about "in the beginning" and the creation of the Universe. John was the apostle "who Jesus loved", who was there at the foot of Jesus' cross comforting Mary as she watched her son die *(John 19:26)*. John was also the apostle who had the honor of writing the Book of Revelation, when the resurrected Jesus appeared to him on the Isle of Patmos, and told him of all the things that were to come. God revealed to John the end from the beginning in the Book of Revelation; but, in the first Chapter of the Book of John, it becomes apparent that God also revealed to John the beginning from the end. The last book John wrote was the revelation of Jesus and the end of time, but the first book John wrote is a revelation of Jesus at the beginning of time. The truths of Genesis 1:1-5 are wonderfully paralleled in the first five verses of the first chapter of the gospel of John making this revelation even clearer:

Genesis 1:1 **In the beginning** God created the heaven and the earth.	John 1:1,2 **In the beginning** was the Word, and the Word was with God, and the Word was God. The same was **in the beginning** with God.
"In the beginning" describes the person Jesus. Substitute "Jesus" for the phrase "in the beginning" when reading these verses.	
Genesis 1:2 And the earth **was** without form, and void; and darkness was upon the face of the deep. And the Spirit of God moved upon the face of the waters.	John 1:3 All things were made by him; and without him was not any thing made that was made.
The Hebrew word *hayah* translated as "was" describes God anticipating the void and darkness and making a way to change this, for not any thing was made except by Him.	
Genesis 1:3 And God said, Let there be light: and there was light.	John 1:4 In him was life; and the life was the light of men.
Jesus Himself said that he is the light of the world and the light of life.	

Genesis 1:4, 5	John 1:5, 12-13
And God saw the light, that it was *good: and God divided the light from the darkness. And God called the light Day and the darkness he called Night*	*The light shines in darkness; and the darkness comprehended it not....But as many as received him, to them gave He power to become the sons of God,* even *to them that believe on his name: Which were born, not of blood, nor of the will of the flesh, nor of the will of man, but of God.*
Badal, translated "divided" means bought or sold. Jesus purchased us with His own blood, and gave us the power to become the sons of God.	
Genesis 5(b)	John 1:14
...the evening and the morning were the first day.	And the Word was made flesh, and dwelt among us, (and we beheld his glory, the glory as of the only begotten of the Father,) full of grace and truth
The first day is the reign of the King, full of glory, grace and truth.	

Jesus, in oneness with his Father, created the heavens and earth, preparing a place where Jesus would live with His Bride. Created man was not that Bride. God Himself came to the earth as a man, died on the cross to become the first born again being, not created, but fashioned and formed by the very Spirit of God. Likewise, when created man chooses Jesus as his Lord, he too becomes born again, no longer a created being, but one formed and fashioned by the Spirit of God, the same Spirit that breathed life into Jesus and raised Him from the dead. Mankind's destiny is not to return to the Garden to walk and talk with God in the cool of the day. Mankind's destiny, planned by God before the foundation of the world, is to become a new being, formed and fashioned from

Jesus, His *ezer kenegdo*, His counterpart, His equal, His Bride. He wanted a Bride, and He is coming for her soon.

> *The one who is testifying to these things says, "Yes, I am coming soon!"*
>
> *Amen! Come, Lord Jesus! (Revelation 22:20, ISV)*

ACCEPTING YOUR MARRIAGE PROPOSAL

The Bride price has been paid for you with the precious life and blood of Jesus. The Ketubah, the marriage contract, the Word of God – every page of your Bible – has been written for you. The skin of wine has been presented.

If you do not yet know Jesus as His Ezer Kenegdo and are not yet betrothed to Him, one thing remains – that you "drink the cup." This simply means that you acknowledge that the price has been paid for YOU, that the written "contract" is His pledge and promise to you, and that He desires more than anything that you "drink the cup" of acceptance.

Many Christian books and pamphlets contain prayers you can pray to accept the marriage proposal. Friends, family, and ministers can have you repeat a prayer after them. These things are fine, but please know that just as a woman chooses her own words to accept a man's proposal, you can do likewise to accept the proposal that Jesus is making to you at this moment. You may respond with a simple "Yes, Lord," or you may want to utter a few sentences from the depths of your heart, or perhaps an abundance of love-laden words will flow from your spirit to your lips to the ears and heart of your newfound Love. However you like, simply talk to the One who is pursuing you, longing for you to be His Bride. Remember, HE WANTED A BRIDE – but not just any bride – He wanted YOU!

Reverend Toni Vidra